TABLE OF CONTENTS

THIS PAGE INTENTIONALLY LEFT BLANK

LIST OF ACRONYMS AND ABBREVIATIONS

AFP   Armed Forces of the Philippines

ARMM   Autonomous Region in Muslim Mindanao

ASG   Abu Sayyaf Group

CIA   Central Intelligence Agency

CPP   Communist Party of the Philippines

DEA   Drug Enforcement Agency

ELN   National Liberation Army

FARC   Revolutionary Armed Forces of Colombia

GoSL   Government of Sri Lanka

GWOT   Global War on Terror

HUKS   Hukbalahap (People's Anti-Japanese Army)

IED   Improvised Explosive Device

IPKF   Indian Peace Keeping Force

JI   Jemaah Islamiyah

JSOTF-P   Joint Special Operations Task Force - Philippines

JTF   Joint Task Force

LTTE   Liberation Tigers of Tamil Eelam

MILF   Moro Islamic Liberation Front

MNLF   Moro National Liberation Front

NPA   New People's Army

PKP   Communist Party of the Philippines

SLA   Sri Lankan Army

SLAF   Sri Lankan Armed Forces

U.S.   United States of America

VBIED   Vehicle Born Improvised Explosive Device

VFA   Visiting Forces Agreement

THIS PAGE INTENTIONALLY LEFT BLANK

ACKNOWLEDGMENTS

The authors wish to thank Dr. Anna Simons for her unwavering support and consistent positive feedback. Her professional guidance allowed us to search beyond our initial objectives and expose us to different ideas by looking at issues through unpopular lenses. We also would like to thank Dr. Gordon McCormick for providing us with a solid foundation of counter-insurgent concepts that helped us during the analytical process of examining insurgencies and foreign governments around the world. A special thanks also goes to COL Brian Greenshields (Ret), whose initial guidance gave us the latitude to explore areas of interest that were important to us. Our thanks are also due to the professors and staff of the Defense Analysis Department, who consistently challenged us to think beyond the academic world. Their insight, expertise, and untiring support have exceeded our expectations for preparing us to return to the Special Operations community.

THIS PAGE INTENTIONALLY LEFT BLANK

I.   INTRODUCTION

In the recent past, there has been an attempt by politicians to justify the need for U.S. armed forces in countries inundated with insurgencies and violent extremist organizations. The idea is that foreign states, volatile or not, may be a breeding ground for terrorism and thus be a danger to the national security of the United States. For example, the Philippines is one country where the U.S. has sent military forces to help eradicate insurgent organizations. Since U.S. forces returned to the Philippines in January 2002, experts, strategists, and senior officials have publicized the counterinsurgency campaign in the Philippines as the most successful effort of the post-9/11 period. Even highly critical nongovernmental organizations have regarded American military efforts as a success story, underscoring the feat of winning hearts and minds through civic action and medical assistance projects.   Philippine Brigadier General Cruz validates these rave reviews by stating that not only has the counterinsurgency campaign reduced the number of communist rebels by 50 percent, the plan has also significantly contributed to the improvement of the business climate and tourism in the provinces.[1]

Although the Philippines may be considered a textbook example of how counterinsurgency operations should be conducted, it is not clear that it offers a template that should be exported. Yes, the Philippines may look good when compared to other conflicts around the world where militaries are struggling to adapt to protracted insurgent warfare. For example, in Afghanistan and Iraq the United States continues to experience extreme levels of difficulty promoting good governance and combating these prolonged insurgencies. American troops are also sustaining significantly higher casualty rates in those two countries compared to the Philippines. However, we broaden our scope of reference from

---

[1] Earth Times, "Military Claims Counterinsurgency Success in Philippines," http://www.earthtimes.org/articles/news/335455,claims-counter-insurgency-success-philippines.html.

1

Afghanistan and Iraq to other contemporary counterinsurgencies, we may discover that there are hidden challenges facing U.S. efforts in the Philippines than we realize.

For instance, the United States' efforts in Colombia may exemplify the kinds of challenges that lie ahead for U.S. endeavors in the Philippines. The U.S. has been involved in Colombian counterinsurgency efforts since the 1950s with recent limited successes. It was not until 1999 that a formal plan was introduced to target the ongoing drug trade and defeat insurgent organizations. Disappointingly, the plan has yet to meet its objectives after more than a decade since implementation. Nor is there a clear or definitive end in sight.

Sri Lanka, on the other hand, offers an example of how a state can defeat an insurgency with little to no help from the U.S. Sri Lanka received varying levels of international support (both civic and military) throughout its 26-year conflict against secessionist insurgents. Towards the end of the conflict, countries such as China and Pakistan contributed greatly to Sri Lanka's success: However, also worth noting is that Sri Lanka's counterinsurgency efforts did involve various levels of human rights violations.

In an attempt to determine whether a U.S. military presence is necessary to defeat insurgencies in the Philippines, we examine the cases of Sri Lanka, Colombia, and the Philippines in greater detail. The Sri Lankan war offers an example of a state that received extremely limited U.S. support to counter a violent secessionist campaign; Colombia's conflict with its guerrillas and drug trade, in contrast, represents a state that has obtained considerable and extended support from the U.S. to battle a Marxist-Leninist revolutionary guerrilla organization; and lastly, the case of the Philippines highlights a state that continues to receive extensive support from Washington as it combats multiple Muslim and communist insurgencies.

In each of our case studies, we seek to examine relationships among insurgent activity, government actions, and U.S. involvement in order to determine whether U.S. presence is necessary to defeat insurgencies in the Philippines. Approaching our cases historically, we will evaluate how Sri Lanka was able to eliminate its insurgency with minimal and eventually no U.S. support, and how continued U.S. support in Colombia has influenced its ability to combat insurgent and drug-related problems. By analyzing the similarities and differences among our cases, we will then be able to weigh whether or not the U.S. presence continues to be necessary in the Philippines.

THIS PAGE INTENTIONALLY LEFT BLANK

II. CASE STUDY: SRI LANKA[2]

A. INTRODUCTION

Sri Lanka, a country in danger of losing its democratic identity, recently brought to an end an ethnically charged civil war that lasted over 26 years. This setting offers an excellent case for studying the influences of competing international intercession. During the last three decades, the Sri Lankan government (GoSL) engaged in a bitter struggle against the Liberation Tigers of Tamil Eelam (LTTE), also known as the Tamil Tigers. Throughout this long war, several nations, including India, Norway, France, and even the U.S., provided varying levels of aid. At the height of the war, however, it was the support from Russia, Iran, Pakistan, and especially the military assistance from China that allowed the GoSL to defeat its adversaries.[3] At the same time, it was the disregard of human rights by both parties that gained international attention and brought outcries from across the globe.

In order to evaluate this scenario, this chapter addresses the Government of Sri Lanka's extended struggle to suppress the Tamil Tigers' volatile revolution. This decades-long struggle is divided into six periods representing the different phases of the war and the brief periods of peace in between. Civil and military contributions by the international community and key events during these periods illustrate the effect that externally involved states have on the outcome of a

---

[2] This chapter draws primarily from the following resources: Robert J. Conner Jr., "Defeating the Modern Asymmetric Threat," Naval Postgraduate School, (2002), http://www.dtic.mil/cgi-bin/GetTRDoc?AD=ADA405818&Location=U2&doc=GetTRDoc.pdf; Mark Kaperak, "Battle of Wills: Accepting Stalemate in Internal Wars. " Naval Postgraduate School, (December 2009), http://www.dtic.mil/cgi-bin/GetTRDoc?AD=ADA514265&Location=U2&doc=GetTRDoc.pdf; "Sri Lanka." Central Intelligence Agency: The World Factbook. https://www.cia.gov/search?q=sri+lanka&x=0&y=0&site=CIA&output=xml_no_dtd&client=CIA&myAction=%2Fsearch&proxystylesheet=CIA&submitMethod=get.Chris Smith, "The Eelam Endgame?" International Affairs, 83 (2007): 1, 69-86; Sri Lanka Virtual Library, (2004), http://www.lankalibrary.com.

[3] R.N. Das, "China's Foray into Sri Lanka and India's Response," Institute for Defense Studies & Analyses, (August 5, 2010), http://www.idsa.in/idsacomments/ChinasForayintoSriLankaandIndiasResponse_rndas_050810.

country's internal conflicts. In turn, these examples may help suggest new parameters for how to determine appropriate levels of involvement by the U.S. in the Philippines as the U.S. attempts to assist the government there.

B.   HISTORICAL BACKGROUND

The beginning of this modern civil war dates back to between five to three centuries before the birth of Christ when the Sinhalese, from northern India, and the Tamils, from southern India, migrated to the island and began their fight for control. The island's history of migration, trade, and colonial invasion led to the formation of a variety of ethnic groups, each with its own language and religious traditions. In addition to the majority Sinhala Buddhists, the country also includes Sri Lankan Tamils, Tamils of recent Indian origin, Muslims, and Burghers (descendants of intermarriages between Sri Lankans and Europeans). Although members of these groups share many cultural practices, beliefs, and values, ethnic differences have become especially significant since the nation's independence in 1948. These differences and the exclusivist policies practiced by the Sinhala-dominated central government led to escalating ethnic conflicts, culminating in the recent civil war. During this war Sri Lankan Tamil rebels fought for an independent nation in the northern and eastern regions of Sri Lanka (which they wanted renamed Eelam).

In 1931, Britain allowed the local population a degree of self-government and sixteen years later, granted the island of Ceylon its independence. The new government leaned towards socialism and promoted Sinhalese interests. It made Sinhalese the national language and effectively reserved the best jobs for the Sinhalese. The move was meant to level the playing field between the majority Sinhalese and the English-speaking, Christian-educated elite; however, this 'affirmative action' also worried the Tamil Hindu minority, which began to press for greater autonomy in the main Tamil areas of the north and east. The country's ethnic and religious conflicts escalated as competition for wealth and work intensified. When Prime Minister Solomon Bandaranaike was assassinated in

6

1959 over his efforts to try to reconcile the two communities, his widow, Sirimavo, succeeded him, becoming the first woman in the world to hold the job of prime minister. A year later, she became the first woman in the world to win a national election. Her government was defeated in 1964, but she returned as prime minister in 1970. Sirimavo maintained close ties with China and then-Indian Prime Minister Indira Gandhi and moved her country to the left politically. In 1972, she declared the country a republic and changed its name to the Democratic Socialist Republic of Sri Lanka.

By the 1970s, tensions between the majority Sinhalese and minority Tamils were escalating. Civil unrest led to a state of emergency in Tamil areas, and a Tamil secessionist movement emerged. The Tamil New Tigers militia, formed in 1972, sought an independent homeland for ethnic Tamils from the north and east. Four years later, the group changed its name to the Liberation Tigers of Tamil Eelam (LTTE), commonly known as the Tamil Tigers.

C.   EELAM WAR I (1983–1987)

An LTTE ambush against a Sri Lankan Army (SLA) patrol (named "Four Four Bravo") in 1983 triggered the start of the 26-year-long war. Singhalese civilians retaliated against innocent Tamils, resulting in massive riots known as "Black July." One of the more noteworthy attacks of Black July took place at Welikada prison during two days of massacre (July 25 and 27).[4] Sinhalese convicts slaughtered 53 Tamil prisoners, most of whom had simply been detained under the Prevention of Rebels Act.[5] Around 50,000 southern Tamil refugees fled as a result of July's bloody conflict, centered mostly in Colombo.[6] Following the riots, the GoSL took measures to relocate the displaced Tamils to

---

[4] "Government Yet to Pay Compensation to July '83 Victims." Daily News. (March 30, 2004). http://www.dailynews.lk/2004/03/30/new14.html.

[5] "The Sri Lanka Project: Massacre in the Hills," *British Refugee Council: No. 153*, (October 2000), http://brcslproject.gn.apc.org/slmonitor/october2000/mass.html.

[6] Edgar O'Balance, *The Cyanide War: Tamil Insurrection in Sri Lanka, 1973-1988*, (London: Brassey's, 1989), 24.

7

northern Sri Lanka, resulting in yet greater hatred of the government and a broadening fissure between the two nations. It is estimated that 1,000 Tamil people were killed,[7] tens of thousands of houses were destroyed and their owners displaced, and a massive wave of Sri Lankan Tamils escaped to other countries.

The violence continued and escalated for two years until, in 1985, the two sides engaged in peace talks in the hopes of achieving a resolution. These negotiations eventually crumbled, resulting in continued hostilities. After prolonged fighting, the LTTE was eventually beaten back to Jaffna, the northern tip of Sri Lanka. As a consequence of internal pressures and outcries from Indian Tamils, India called for a cessation of the GoSL's offensive. The Sri Lankan government dismissed India's pleas and continued its attack. India then attempted to aid the LTTE with supplies, and was eventually successful with airdrops.

Hesitant of further antagonizing India, the Sri Lankan President agreed to peace talks monitored by the Indian government. As a result of the ensuing peace talks, the GoSL lifted its siege on Jaffna and, along with the Indian Prime Minister, signed the Indo-Sri-Lankan Accord on July 29, 1987.

D.   INDO-SRI LANKAN PEACE ACCORD (1987–1990)

In agreement with the Indo-Sri-Lanka Accord, India committed soldiers to aid in monitoring and maintaining the agreement between the GoSL and the LTTE.   The 80,000 man Indian Peace Keeping Force (IPKF) deployed to Sri Lanka from 1987 to 1990. As part of the accord, LTTE fighters were required to lay down their arms before receiving local power from the GoSL and official status for the Tamil language. Additionally, India was to cease support of the Tamil Tigers and recognize Sri Lanka's unity.

---

[7] "President Kumaratunga's speech on the 21st Anniversary of 'Black July,' Presidential Secretariat, Colombo, July 23, 2004," South Asia Terrorism Portal, (July 23, 2004). http://www.satp.org/satporgtp/countries/shrilanka/document/papers/BlackJuly2004.htm.

Old hatreds and mistrust, however, continued to poison the possibility of peace, and all three sides struggled to honor the arrangement. As the SLA and LTTE's retaliations continued to escalate, the IPKF was drawn further into the conflict. The IPKF and the LTTE engaged in no less than five significant engagements. By the time the IPKF completely withdrew in 1990, the IPKF had suffered approximately 1,255 killed in action and several thousand wounded.[8]

E.   EELAM WAR II (1990–1995)

As peace disintegrated, the LTTE strength and violence amplified. The catalyst that kicked off a new chapter in the war happened on June 10, 1990, when the LTTE attacked, captured, and massacred nearly 600 police officers in eastern Sri Lanka. Throughout this phase of the war, each faction claimed victories; in reality, however, the damages were taking a heavy toll on both sides.

In May 1991, the LTTE carried out a devastating attack in Colombo killing the Indian Prime Minister, Rajiv Gandhi, and 13 civilians. Gandhi's assassination was intended to be payback for the IPKF attacks against the Tamils and India's withdrawal of support from the LTTE. Not surprisingly, however, the LTTE's actions only succeeded in alienating Indian Tamil support.

In 1994, Chandrika Kumaratunga was elected president of Sri Lanka. Almost immediately, President Kumaratunga entered into peace talks with LTTE leader Velupillai Prabhakaran. In January 1995, the "Cessation of Hostilities Agreement" was signed. This time, the cease-fire lasted approximately four months before the LTTE conducted two attacks, killing two SLA soldiers and destroying two Sri Lankan Navy gunboats.

F.   EELAM WAR III (1995–2001)

In the third phase of this protracted war, the LTTE again intensified its use of violence, utilizing surface-to-air missiles against the Sri Lankan Air Force. In

---

[8] "IPKF in Sri Lanka – India's Vietnam." Sri Lanka Virtual Library. (March 2000). http://www.lankalibrary.com/pol/india3.htm.

desperate need of defensive measures, the GoSL began seeking increased aid from international sources. In retaliation for the onslaught of LTTE attacks against its interests, the SLA conducted a massive push into the Tamil-controlled northern area. But now, the LTTE had had time to grow its troop strength and logistics capabilities and was able to repel the SLA attack. President Kumaratunga attempted to readdress reconciliation and a peace agreement with the LTTE; Prabhakaran rejected his terms and ratcheted up his attacks.

The LTTE hijacked a civilian cruise ship in August of 1995 and from the end of 1995 to the beginning of 1996, the SLA forced its way into the Jaffna Peninsula, displacing all civilians from the cities into the jungle. The Eelam War III was marked by a continuous escalation of violence by both sides, with the LTTE bringing the fight closer to Colombo, overrunning SLA camps and police stations, staging an unsuccessful assassination attempt against President Kumaratunga, and launching a truck bomb attack against the Buddhist Sacred Temple of the Tooth (said to house a tooth from the Buddha). In 1997, the U.S. placed the LTTE on its list of Foreign Terrorist Organizations and finally, at the end of 2000, after six years of brutal fighting, both sides broke down and agreed to another ceasefire agreement, this time brokered by a Norwegian delegation.

Shortly after the 2000 truce, however, both sides broke the ceasefire agreement, leading once again to hostilities. The LTTE conducted an attack at the Colombo International Airport, destroying eight Sri Lankan Air Force planes, three civilian planes, and damaging five others, thereby crippling Sri Lanka's tourism industry. The war continued until elections in December of 2001 helped the GoSL and LTTE return to their ceasefire agreement. This time, Prabhakaran compromised on his goal of complete Tamil autonomy and offered to settle for regional autonomy, with the Tamils to be granted control over the politics and economy in their region. A few months later on February 22, 2002, the GoSL and

LTTE signed the Norwegian Peace Accord, withdrawing combat forces behind technical control lines monitored by the Norwegian-led Sri Lankan Monitoring Mission.[9]

G.   NORWEGIAN ACCORD (2002–2005)

As the Norwegian Peace Accord went into effect, the GoSL and LTTE technical control lines morphed into borders and the LTTE gradually built a Tamil state. From 2002 until 2005, the LTTE maintained control of a Tamil autonomous zone, complete with police, a functioning judicial system, social welfare services and economic development (in close conjunction with numerous non-governmental organizations), and an external security apparatus in the form of the LTTE, which provided a check against the traditional threat posed by the GoSL and SLAF.[10]

Unfortunately, despite the potential for a lasting peace in Sri Lanka, several factors led to the breakdown of the Norway-brokered ceasefire agreement. Notably, the question of authorities for development and humanitarian relief in Tamil-held areas created fear among some Sinhalese politicians about the possible institutionalization of power-sharing arrangements between the GoSL and Tamils that would undermine the sovereignty of the Sri Lankan unitary state.[11] This issue came to a head in the aftermath of the 2004 tsunami, which killed some 30,000 Sri Lankans, when disputes erupted over the allocation and flow of relief aid in the Tamil state.[12] As humanitarian assistance flowed into Sri Lanka from around the world, little of it reached the Tamils. The

---

[9] Damien Kingsbury, "Sri Lanka," In *Hot Spot: Asia and Oceania* by Clinton Fernandes, (Westport: Greenwood Press, 2008), 234.

[10] Kristian Stokke, "Building the Tamil Eelam State: Emerging State Institutions and Forms of Governance in LTTE-controlled Areas in Sri Lanka," *Third World Quarterly,* 27 no. 6 (2006), 1021–1040.

[11] Kristian Stokke, "Building the Tamil Eelam State: Emerging State Institutions and Forms of Governance in LTTE-controlled Areas in Sri Lanka," *Third World Quarterly,* 27 no. 6 (2006), 1021–1040.

[12] Damien Kingsbury, "Sri Lanka," In *Hot Spot: Asia and Oceania* by Clinton Fernandes, (Westport: Greenwood Press, 2008), 235.

LTTE used this disparity to call for a boycott of the 2005 presidential elections, which "assisted in the defeat of the pro-peace candidate and the election of the more belligerent Mahinda Rajapaksa."[13]

H.   EELAM WAR IV (2006–2009)

The LTTE and the GoSL blamed each other for violations of the ceasefire agreement and the subsequent return to war. In August 2005, the LTTE allegedly assassinated Sri Lankan foreign minister, Laxman Kadirgamar, an ethnic Tamil who had a reputation for lobbying the international community for proscription of the LTTE. On the GoSL side, a change in policies led to widespread unlawful detentions and the disappearance of Tamils, stoking what was already long-standing animosity between the two sides. In the early part of 2006, bilateral talks in Geneva broke down over accusations of ceasefire violations by both sides, and by the middle of 2006 approximately 1,000 lives had been lost in conflict-related incidents.

The LTTE returned to suicide bombings, killing the third highest-ranking SLA officer and bringing more violence to Colombo. For the GoSL and the SLAF, the failure of the ceasefire agreement delivered them their final opportunity to destroy the LTTE. From 2006–2009, the SLA brought the full power of the military to bear against the LTTE. Combined with help from splintering Tamil factions and the GoSL emergency regulations, which restricted open media coverage and led to countless unwarranted detentions, the SLA militarily defeated the LTTE in 2009, killing as many as 20,000 civilians in the final months

---

13 Damien Kingsbury, "Sri Lanka," In *Hot Spot: Asia and Oceania* by Clinton Fernandes, (Westport: Greenwood Press, 2008), 235.

of the conflict.[14] On May 18, 2009, the SLA killed Velupillai Prabhakaran andother key LTTE leaders, dealing a crippling blow to the LTTE and delivering a major success for the GoSL.[15]

In the wake of this, it is not clear what the future holds for the Tamils in Sri Lanka. The SLA did defeat the LTTE on the battlefield: However, in the process it displaced several hundred thousand Tamils, holding them in government internment camps while it allegedly searched for remaining members of the LTTE.[16]

I. SUMMARY

For more than three decades, the LTTE battled against the GoSL for Tamil autonomy. This insurgency was protracted in the sense that the LTTE's determination to fight never wavered; however, the level of violence the LTTE employed against the GoSL quickly escalated during each phase of the conflict. With each side battling for its survival and with varying degrees of external support affecting the conflict, neither side was willing to concede its values or goals to the other. In some ways, then, the Sri Lankan civil war demonstrates what happens when political will is galvanized and neither side proves willing to compromise: over 30 years of violence.

When one looks at the level of violence in each phase of the LTTE's war against the GoSL, it seems apparent that whenever violence increased in intensity and proximity to Colombo, the GoSL was more determined to end the conflict. The fact that as violence increased in general in Sri Lanka, the GoSL took actions to suppress it can also be attributed to the relatively small physical size of the country. A violent attack anywhere on the island could cumulatively

---

14 Robert D. Kaplan, "To Catch a Tiger," *The Atlantic.* (July 1, 2009), http://www.theatlantic.com/doc/200907u/tamil-tigers-counterinsurgency.

15 "Sri Lanka: The End of the Tigers," STRATFOR Global Intelligence, http://www.stratfor.com.libproxy.nps.edu/analysis/20090518_sri_lanka_end_tigers.

16 Robert Templar, "War Without End," *International Herald Tribune,* (July 21, 2009), http://www.nytimes.com/2009/07/22/opinion/22iht-edtempler.html.

contribute to the political effect of increased the desire to end the violence. As LTTE attacks increased in general throughout the island and against the SLAF, GoSL resolve to defeat the LTTE also increased.

III. CASE STUDY: COLOMBIA

A. INTRODUCTION

The United States has provided varying levels of support to combat Colombia's adversaries. As early as the mid-1800s, U.S. troops suppressed multiple rebellions in Colombian-owned Panama. A century later, the U.S. was still providing assistance to this Latin American country: in the 1960s, the U.S. provided counterinsurgency experts to help facilitate the elimination of communist insurgents; in the 1970s, the U.S. helped initiate a war on drugs to debilitate insurgents using drug trafficking to finance their operations; and, since 9/11, the U.S. has contributed to Colombia's efforts to defeat threats of terrorism.

Despite America's history of support for Colombia, critics argue that U.S. involvement in Colombian affairs actually helps feed rather than mitigate internal conflict. In order to evaluate this argument, this chapter addresses four interrelated time periods that involve direct U.S. assistance: La Violencia (1948-1958), insurgencies (1960s to present), drug trade (1970s to present), and Plan Colombia (1999 to present). The United States' participation in key events during these periods may help establish whether U.S. involvement in Colombian affairs actually improve or exacerbate Colombia's internal conflict.

B. HISTORICAL BACKGROUND

Despite a history of diplomatic relationships dating back to the early 19th century, U.S.-Colombian affairs have fluctuated between cordial and controversial. Although the U.S. honored 1856 treaty obligations by deploying U.S. troops to help suppress multiple Colombian rebellions, the Colombian senate refused to ratify a 1903 treaty,[17] which provoked the U.S. to encourage

---

[17] The 1903 Treaty (Hay-Herran Treaty) would have allowed the United States complete ownership and control of the Panama Canal.

the Panamanians to secede from Colombia. The conflict proved to be fruitful for the U.S. when the newly established country of Panama agreed to have the U.S. construct and operate the Panama Canal.

In 1928, positive U.S.-Colombian ties were confirmed when Colombian armed forces mobilized to protect a U.S. business that was being threatened. Employees of a U.S.-owned banana plantation were conducting a strike to improve work conditions. Colombian troops shot more than 1,000 plantation workers, women, and children. This event, known as the United Banana Massacre, demonstrated the government's willingness to use aggression to resolve conflict. Moreover, it incited a belief among Colombians that the government was more interested in protecting U.S. interests than those of its own citizens. While the government managed to maintain control after the eruption of a violent revolt in 1928,[18] the United Banana Massacre marked the beginning of the turn to violence.

C.   LA VIOLENCIA (1948–1958)

The event that ushered in an entire decade of violent civil conflict, known as La Violencia, was the 1948 assassination of presidential candidate and leader of the Liberal Party, Jorge Gaitan.[19] Gaitan's murder provoked a massive uprising, known as El Bogotazo, in the capital city of Bogota, which consisted of vicious riots between liberal and conservative political parties.[20] The violence that took the lives of 3,000 to 5,000 individuals and injured thousands more, eventually spread to the rural countryside. Rural communities witnessed brutal clashes between Liberal and Conservative peasants battling for rights to land. Armed death squads were also known to travel to various parts of the country to conduct horrific killings of their opponents to include cutting testicles, slashing the

---

[18] Caterine LeGrand, "Agrarian Antecedents of Violence," in *Violence in Colombia: The Contemporary Crisis in Historical Perspective,* ed. Charles Berquist, Richard Penaranda, and Gonzalo Sanchez, 31–42 (Wilmington: A Scholarly Resources Inc., 1992).

[19] Geoff Simons, *Colombia: A Brutal History,* (London: SAQI, 2004) 40.

[20] Geoff Simons, *Colombia: A Brutal History,* (London: SAQI, 2004) 40.

bellies of pregnant women, and stabbing babies with bayonets.[21] It was also during this time that one of the nastiest signatures of death was invented, the Colombian necktie, which later became the trademark of drug kingpin killings.[22]

The level of violence grew so significantly that the only way to quell the insurrection was to employ military forces, and although most armed groups (called bandoleros) were demobilized by 1953, not all were. Conditions began to change in 1957, however, when moderate Liberals and Conservatives agreed to form a bipartisan alliance, known as the Nation Front, with the intent to end years of bloody political violence. Over the course of a decade, La Violencia claimed the lives of over 200,000 Colombians.

Despite this dark period in Colombian history, the U.S. government expanded its national interests beyond the Panamanian isthmus and took a keen interest in the country's agri-business. The U.S. helped finance local farming companies to exploit the oil reserves in the region and siphon oil revenue into the U.S. economy. This monetary assistance eventually forced the Colombian government to rely on additional support from the U.S.-dominated World Bank. Due to its enormous debt to the U.S., Colombia felt obliged to commit a battalion of troops and a naval vessel in support of the Korean War. Continued efforts to bolster relations between the U.S. and Colombia served as a link on which the future partnership to combat Colombia's rising insurgent problem would be built.

D.   INSURGENCIES (1960s–PRESENT)

The end of La Violencia was not the end of armed peasant groups. Many peasant groups remained united in enclaves throughout the country. While the Colombian government believed these groups were a threat to the state, the U.S. considered them a threat to U.S. business interests. In order to help counter the threat, the U.S. sent a United States Special Forces Advisory team to help the

---

[21] Geoff Simons, *Colombia: A Brutal History,* (London: SAQI, 2004) 40–41.

[22] Geoff Simons, *Colombia: A Brutal History,* (London: SAQI, 2004) 41.

Colombian government identify its internal security needs. Three years later, the U.S. sent another team of counterinsurgency experts who recommended the initiation of Colombia's Internal Defense Plan (code name Plan Lazo) to destroy communist insurgents. Although Plan Lazo was based on a carrot and stick model, civic action programs (e.g., building homes and roads, organizing youth camps, and providing university grants) were often overshadowed by vicious military operations. For example, aircraft would drop napalm on peasant enclaves to eliminate the threat. In other instances, hunter killer teams would strap dead bandoleros to helicopters' landing gear and fly over towns to publicize military success. Despite making considerable military headway, hostile efforts by government forces to destroy all remaining bandoleros reignited the violence, which resulted in the creation of several communist guerrilla movements.

Two significant communist guerrilla organizations emerged during Colombia's political chaos and, to this day, continue to challenge the state for political control: the National Liberation Army (ELN)[23] and the Revolutionary Armed Forces of Colombia (FARC). Although the ELN continues to execute brutal attacks and countless number of abductions against civilian targets, it is less well known that the more prominent FARC.

Officially formed in the 1960s, the FARC is considered to be one of the oldest and largest revolutionary guerrilla movements in the Western Hemisphere and the longest lived guerrilla movement in Latin America. Although it is best known as a terror organization funded through drug trade and kidnappings, its origins lie in protecting the rural poor from state military aggression. In order to financially support measures to protect the repressed populace from the long arm of the government, the FARC 'taxed' various institutions (cattle ranchers, energy companies, and oil producers) through extortion and kidnapping for ransom.

While the FARC went through growing pains in the 1960s and 1970s, the 1980s proved to be a time of unification. The beginning of the decade was

---

[23] ELN stands for Ejercito de Liberacion Nacional.

marked by a series of negotiations between the communist organization and the government, resulting in a 1984 peace agreement: However, the government failed to follow through on many of its promises. The situation worsened in 1985 when government-sponsored paramilitary groups killed a significant number of guerrilla leaders. Fortunately for the FARC, atrocities being committed by the drug cartels diverted the attention of the government, allowing guerrilla forces to consolidate and reorganize.

Similarly, the 1990s began with peace talks. The FARC, however, continued to carry out hostilities against the Colombian government, security forces, and civilians who opposed their cause. In 1994, the FARC attempted to disrupt congressional and presidential elections by engaging in more kidnappings. The kidnapping of two American missionaries demonstrated the group's disapproval of U.S. involvement in Colombian affairs. As a consequence of the group's failure to stop its criminal activities while it was at the negotiating table, the Colombian army responded with frequent attacks against the communist rebels. In reaction, the FARC launched its own attacks against the Colombian army from 1996 to 1998.

Under the leadership of President Uribe in the 2000s, the Colombian military and police had tremendous success combating the FARC. Uribe received considerable praise for his resolve to intensify military operations. Nevertheless, regardless of government successes, the FARC managed to respond with its own small-scale counter-attacks. For example, one operation in 2003 resulted in the assassination of a regional governor, a former defense minister, and eight soldiers; a year later, the group massacred seven peasants; and in 2005, the FARC conducted multiple attacks accounting for more than 40 deaths.

The 2000s also saw a significant rise in kidnap operations. Whereas some kidnappings were intended to facilitate the negotiation of prisoner exchanges, others were conducted for extortion. Similarly, while some kidnappings ended peacefully (like the 2006 release of a German citizen after five years of captivity), others ended more violently (like the 2002 kidnapping of 12 provincial deputies that resulted in 11 dead hostages in 2007). The kidnapping that gained the most notoriety occurred in 2002 when FARC guerrillas abducted presidential candidate Ingrid Betancourt. One result of this kidnapping was the subsequent rescue operation in 2008 to free Betancourt and 15 other hostages: The entire operation was planned and directed by senior Colombian officials (with minor assistance from U.S. advisors), and entirely executed by Colombian military forces.

Given Colombia's struggle against guerrillas over the past 50 years, the United States has continued sending support to Colombia to help improve its state of security affairs. For example, in 1961, President Kennedy visited Bogota to demonstrate the U.S.'s commitment to restoring state legitimacy. Although Kennedy was greeted by a cheering crowd, he was shocked to discover that the people thought he was there in support of the peasants, not the oppressive oligarchs (government, military, and elites).[24] Despite this initial misperception, the U.S. proceeded to pursue the improvement of Colombian governance and suppress the communist movements. To achieve these objectives, the U.S. assumed multiple roles: counterinsurgency experts helped conduct clandestine activities in guerrilla controlled areas in order to undermine communist influence, military advisors influenced the hiring and firing of senior military leaders, and technical specialists employed "black propaganda"[25] through church radio broadcasts to shape the attitudes and behavior of various target audiences. In spite of varying levels of success, U.S. assistance eventually faced significant challenges thanks to the severe escalation in the drug trade.

---

[24] Geoff Simons, *Colombia: A Brutal History,* (London: SAQI, 2004) 48.

[25] U.S. agencies would broadcast messages under the guise of other organizations. They instructed peasants to organize local self-defense programs to protect their families and communities from guerrilla harassment.

E. DRUG TRADE (1970–PRESENT)

The drug trade in Colombia gained notoriety the 1970s with the formation and activities of the Medellin Cartel[26] (led by the ruthless Pablo Escobar), but it rose to even greater prominence with the exploits of the Cali[27] and Norte del Valle[28] Cartels. Although peasants and lower class citizens initially viewed the cartels as groups that wanted to improve conditions for the people, the cartels quickly resorted to terror tactics to coerce the populace in supporting their operations. To further complicate things, corrupt Colombian law enforcement officials and legislators would facilitate drug operations in various ways.

Colombian drug cartels proved to be violent and merciless drug organizations. They were structured in such a way that only members with family in Colombia would be allowed to handle sensitive operations. This practice permitted cartels access to family members as a type of insurance to prevent members from going to the authorities. The cartels were also known for using different levels of violence. In some cases, the threat of violence was sufficient; however, in other instances, extreme brutality was necessary. For example, the "Minister of War" for one cartel directed the slaughter of 100 people by chain saw. Another example is the beheading of a person who merely denounced the actions of the cartel.

Beyond the violent nature of the cartels, U.S. and Colombian government officials were concerned with the large-scale production and distribution of illegal drugs. As early as the 1970s, 90 percent of marijuana sold in the United States came from Colombia, while 70 percent of cocaine imported into the United States originated from Colombia. The sudden increase of the drug trade in the 1970s

---

[26] The Medellin Cartel was an extremely violent organization that would not hesitate to kill anyone who interfered with its objectives: government officials, politicians, law enforcement officials, journalists, and innocent bystanders.

[27] The Cali Cartel originally began as a kidnapping ring and transitioned to drug trafficking (first marijuana, then cocaine).

[28] The Norte del Valle Cartel was known as one of the most powerful organizations in the illegal drug trade after the Cali Cartel and Medellin Cartel fragmented.

convinced the U.S. and Colombian governments to expand their relationship to focus on eradicating the production, processing, and trafficking of illegal drugs. Although President Nixon was the first president to declare a "war on drugs" in 1971, the Reagan administration popularized the motto in the 1980s in an effort to thwart the volume of drugs coming into the United States. Despite multiple studies that predicted the use of armed forces would have almost no effect on cocaine imports into the U.S., President George H. W. Bush continued Reagan's anti-drug policy, arguing that in order to completely eradicate narcotics, the source of the drugs needed to be destroyed.

As the war on drugs in Colombia continued into the 1990s, the U.S. Central Intelligence Agency (CIA) and the U.S. Drug Enforcement Agency (DEA) elevated their efforts to combat not only the drug trade, but also the various insurgencies. In 1992, the CIA acknowledged that, although communist guerrillas like the FARC were not "directly" involved in the drug trade, they did use drug trafficking as a source of revenue by taxing drug operations in their areas of control. In 1994, the DEA concurred with the CIA, arguing that Colombia's insurgent organizations were not a primary cause of the drug problem because they did not engage directly in "independent" illicit drug activities.

For the past forty years, the United States has contributed financial, logistical, and tactical aid to Colombia in an effort to combat the illegal drug trade. The prolonged presence of drug cartels in Colombia has compelled the U.S. to continue its partnership with the Colombian government well into the 2000s. The most notable contribution the U.S. has made has been in support of Plan Colombia.

F.   PLAN COLOMBIA (1999–PRESENT)

After decades of aggressive drug cartel operations and violent insurgent activity, the Colombian government devised a strategy named Plan Colombia in 1999 to eradicate both types of groups. Although the original plan under

President Pastrana did not specifically emphasize drug trafficking and military aid, it did seek to destroy drug crops and improve economic conditions, not unlike the post-WWII Marshall Plan. In order to receive significant financial and logistical aid from the U.S., Pastrana had to agree to extensive U.S. inputs, to include bolstering counter-narcotics programs and improving the military.

Despite Pastrana's desire to demonstrate the government's commitment to improve social and economic conditions, his six-phased Plan Colombia[29] was not well received. State officials and citizens alike asserted that the plan was riddled with imperfections. For example, although the final plan appeared to include a comprehensive strategy to combat narco-trafficking, encourage social development, and reform the judicial system, it failed to outline specific measures to address domestic violence and government volatility. Furthermore, in many Colombians' view, there was a correlation between Plan Colombia and the coup in Chile; they believed this policy was a ruse for another war waged by the United States on oil-rich soil. Statistically speaking, this would appear to be borne given U.S. financial aid to Colombia from 1999–2001: military aid accounted for 97 percent of total financial aid in 1999, 78 percent in 2000, and 97 percent in 2001.

Despite grievances from critics, the U.S. continued to support Plan Colombia: U.S. Army Special Forces resumed working with the Colombian military to retake territory controlled by the FARC and drug cartels, and President Bush advocated additional financial, material, and intelligence support so long as the Colombian people were willing to fight for their own country.[30] Even with U.S. backing, however, drug trafficking continued.

The United States remained influential with the Colombian government after the 2002 presidential elections. The United States Congress encouraged newly elected President Alvaro Uribe Velez to intensify counter-narcotics

---

[29] Connie Veillette, "Plan Colombia: A Progress Report," Report for Congress, June 22, 2005, http://www.fas.org/sgp/crs/row/RL32774.pdf.

[30] Garbriel Marcella, "The United States and Colombia: The Journey from Ambiguity to Strategic Clarity," May 2003, http://www.strategicstudiesinstitute.army.mil/pubs/display.cfm?pubID=10.

operations and expand these efforts to include terror organizations.[31] During his two terms as president, Uribe was instrumental in promoting Plan Colombia. In addition to stabilizing the economy, Uribe focused Colombia's efforts on destroying coca cultivation, which would undercut the illicit drug trade, and thereby disrupt a major source of the insurgents' funding. His goal was to make insurgents less capable of carrying out operations and force them to meet state demands.[32] Due to the successes of Plan Colombia and an apparent decline in FARC numbers and capabilities, the plan was renewed after its initial six years.

G.   SUMMARY

For the past fifty years, Colombia has been inundated with political controversy, violent insurgent activity, and vicious drug trafficking. Each of these problems has impacted both foreign and domestic U.S. interests. As such, the U.S. government has contributed substantial time, money, and resources to help Colombia resolve its many challenges. Despite decades of assistance, the single most productive contribution has been the U.S.'s support of Plan Colombia. Plan Colombia's spectrum of vital concerns has largely been successful; however, the six-phase plan has yet to be fully realized. After ten years, Colombia has only just reached Phase Four. Recognizing this fact, the U.S. must constantly question how much more it will contribute in the future and how much longer its efforts are going to be required before the U.S. can conclude its prolonged involvement in Colombia.

---

[31] Maria Clemencia Ramirez, "Maintaining Democracy in Colombia through Political Exclusion, Sate of Exception, Counterinsurgency, and Dirty War," In *Violent Democracies in Latin America*, ed. Enrique Desomnd Arias and Daniel M. Goldstein, 84–107, (Durham: Duke University Press, 2010) 95.

[32] Maria Clemencia Ramirez, "Maintaining Democracy in Colombia through Political Exclusion, Sate of Exception, Counterinsurgency, and Dirty War," In *Violent Democracies in Latin America*, ed. Enrique Desomnd Arias and Daniel M. Goldstein, 84–107, (Durham: Duke University Press, 2010) 96.

IV.   CASE STUDY: PHILIPPINES[33]

A.   INTRODUCTION

The United States has played a fundamental role combating enemies of the Philippines: in 1898, the United States declared war on Spain; during World War II, American armed forces fought against the Japanese Empire; immediately following Philippine independence, Americans helped suppress a communist rebellion; and in the 2000s, the United States military assisting the Armed Forces of the Philippines (AFP) to fight against several Islamic insurgencies.   In reference to the long history of fighting Philippine adversaries, there are two views of U.S. involvement.   First, critics argue that American presence encourages and prolongs insurgent activity.   The second view is that U.S. involvement is necessary to help the government defeat its opponents.

In an effort to address these contrary points of view, this chapter identifies four distinct periods of insurgent activity: the initial communist insurgency following World War II (1946–1954), the inception of new insurgencies (1960s–1992), the formation of violent extremist groups (1990s), and the persistence of insurgent activity (2000s).

B.   HISTORICAL BACKGROUND

Even with the arrival of Arab merchants and traders between the twelfth and fourteenth centuries, the Philippines remained relatively peaceful. It was not until the 1500s that the native population rose up against foreign invaders: they revolted against Spanish colonizers, who attempted to impose Roman Catholicism between the sixteenth and the nineteenth centuries, and they also rebelled against the United States, which was accused of disrupting indigenous

---

[33] The facts, figures, and data found within this chapter were taken from the following sources: Federation of American Scientists, http://www.fas.org; Global Security, http://www.globalsecurity.org; Jane's Information Group, http://jtic.janes.com; and "Worldwide Incidents Tracking System," National Counterterrorism Center, http://wits-classic.nctc.gov.

religious and social customs between 1898 and 1946. The populace also periodically rebelled against corrupt governments when they attempted to suppress specific sections of the population both before and after independence. The majority of post-independence conflicts originated from ethnic, culture, social, and religious issues that had been ignored previously resulting in the formation of numerous insurgent groups.

C.   INITIAL INSURGENCY (1946–1954)

Shortly after World War II, the United States granted the Philippines its independence after first imposing a number of controversial economic and military treaties.   For example, the Bell Trade Act of 1946 granted U.S. businesses equal rights to owning land as well as access to natural resources, and the Military Bases Agreement of 1947 granted the United States the right to maintain military bases throughout the country.   These agreements, coupled with government repression and landlord reprisals, fueled a group of communist rebels known as the Hukbalahap (People's Anti-Japanese Army - Huks).

The Huks became the military arm of the Communist Party of the Philippines (PKP) and attempted to overthrow the government.   Grievances against the government included the lack of reforms: land, social, and economic. The Huks originally developed as a guerrilla army in 1942 to fight Japanese invaders.   Due to government corruption and the failure of the Roxas administration to implement sufficient land reforms, they quickly evolved into a violent insurgent group. Despite conducting a wide range of violent actions,[34] the Huks are best known for executing unconventional warfare.

In 1946, the Huks and the PKP began an armed and parliamentary struggle.   While the PKP attempted to use legal channels, the Huks conducted hasty ambushes and raids against small government forces, convoys, and patrols.   By 1948, the Huks intensified their aggression against government

---

[34] The Huks also conducted holdups, robberies, murders, rapes, kidnappings, intimidation, and massacres of small villages.

forces, especially after the PKP decreed that democracy and peace could no longer be achieved through parliamentary struggle. As the Huks grew stronger, American military officials and the Central Intelligence Agency (CIA) used the Joint U.S. Military Advisory Group to assume a significant role in the Philippines' counterinsurgency efforts. The U.S. military's ability to help introduce organizational changes to the Armed Forces of the Philippines (AFP), improve training, and provide better equipment allowed the Secretary of National Defense, Ramon Magsaysay, to employ his own unconventional methods to battle the communist rebels. Magsaysay's success helped transform the population's attitude toward the AFP from one of distrust to admiration. Magsaysay's efforts and several Huks setbacks[35] led to the decline and eventual demise of the Huks in 1954.

It is important to note that the inclusion of the Economic Development Corporation project into the counterinsurgency program greatly contributed to the Huks' demise. The project provided incentives for ex-Huks and supporters of the Huks to own their own land and escape poverty by relocating to the southern Philippines. Although the project helped squelch the communist insurgency, the relocation of predominantly Christian Filipino citizens to a predominantly Muslim region transferred a new problem to the southern Philippines.

D. THE RISE OF INSURGENCIES (1960s–1992)

During President Marcos's dictatorship (1965–1986), government repression, lack of social, economic, land reform, and the imposition of martial law contributed to the rise of multiple insurgent groups. The New People's Army (NPA) was formed in 1969 as the armed wing of the Communist Party of the Philippines (CPP); its aim was to establish a communist government. In contrast, the Moro National Liberation Front's (MNLF) goal was to secede from the

---

[35] The Huks lost significant support beginning with their assassination of President Quezon's widow in 1949, their continued intimidation of the populace, and the surrender of their leader (Luis Taruc) in 1954.

27

Philippines and establish an Islamic state in the southern part of the country; the MNLF was founded in 1972. The Moro Islamic Liberation Front (MILF) then split from the MNLF in 1977 due to differing views on self-rule.

As a result of the rising threat of anarchy and an increase in NPA activities in the early 1970s, Marcos declared martial law in 1972. Although martial law was initially welcomed, government corruption, political repression, and state-sponsored human rights violations soon followed. The NPA reacted in kind by conducting its own human rights violations. The communist rebels were also guilty of extortion and kidnappings, but the majority of their operations consisted of armed attacks against military personnel and government officials. United States personnel were not exempt from NPA targeting. In fact, the communist rebels gained instant notoriety after assassinating U.S. Special Forces advisor Colonel Nick Rowe[36] in 1989.

Various Muslim insurgencies emerged during this period,[37] especially after the 1968 Jabidah Massacre.[38] The MNLF, for example, quickly transformed from a political movement into a militant organization and began carrying out attacks against government forces. In fact, the MNLF aggression (1973–1977) caused the death of more than 13,000 people and forced more than a million people to flee their homes. After carrying out violent counter-measures throughout the 1970s and 1980s (during the Marcos regime), the Philippine government, under the new leadership of President Aquino, eventually acceded to the creation of the Autonomous Region in Muslim Mindanao (ARMM) in 1989. The ARMM allowed the predominantly Muslim regions of the southern Philippines to govern themselves.

---

[36] COL Rowe provided counterinsurgency training to the AFP and worked closely with the CIA to penetrate the NPA.

[37] Muslim Filipinos complained about government discrimination is such areas as housing, education, financial funding, and the relocation project of relocating Christian Filipinos from the northern Philippines to Muslim majority regions of the southern Philippines.

[38] The Jabidah Massacre, also known as the Corregidor Massacre, refers to an incident when the AFP executed at least 28 Muslim army recruits.

In the beginning of the 1990s, insurgent activities directed against U.S. facilities and personnel spiked again. The NPA conducted numerous attacks against multiple U.S. Information Service offices, the American Embassy, and a transmitter tower for the *Voice of America*. In addition to killing two U.S. airmen and a Marine sergeant in two separate incidents, the communist group kidnapped several American citizens.[39] The Aquino administration fought back by raiding NPA safe-houses, implementing reward programs for information leading to the arrest of NPA key leaders, and campaigning against support for the communist movement.

Counterterrorist efforts and the improved political climate under President Aquino greatly contributed to the decrease in terrorist incidents in 1991 and 1992. After taking office in 1992, President Ramos helped further dampen violent insurgent activities by legalizing the CPP, releasing a significant number of communist leaders, and suspending ongoing trials of NPA detainees. Despite the conciliatory efforts made by the government, fratricidal fighting among NPA and CPP members,[40] and an overall decrease in activity, the communist rebels continued to target American military personnel stationed in the Philippines.

E. VIOLENT EXTREMIST GROUPS (1990s)

The threat of attack against U.S. bases and personnel was virtually eliminated after the Philippine government refused to renew the 1947 Military Bases Agreement. The decision not to renew the 25-year-old agreement[41] forced U.S. military personnel to leave the country in 1992[42] and helped the

---

[39] E.g., a businessman, a rancher, and a Peace Corps volunteer.

[40] The internal killing spree was known as the Second Great Rectification Movement and occurred between 1992 and 1998. It involved the internal murders of NPA and CPP members accused of being agents of the AFP and other governmental organizations.

[41] The refusal to renew the Military Bases Agreement led the Americans to cease almost all substantial U.S. military aid packages to the Philippines, which frequently exceeded $100 million but dwindled to almost nothing.

[42] Base closures included Clark Air Base, which was declared a total loss after the eruption of Mount Pinatubo, Subic Bay Naval Station, and more than twenty smaller military facilities.

Philippines regain trust with its neighbors throughout Southeast Asia. The withdrawal of U.S. personnel marked the first time since the 1500s that no foreign military forces were present in the Philippines.

Shortly after U.S. military forces departed the Philippines, peace negotiations resumed between the Philippine government and the MNLF. Both sides finally reached a compromise in 1996, ending the MNLF's 24-year long insurgency against the state. However, despite reaching a peace agreement with the MNLF, the government faced the formation of two new Islamic insurgent groups: Jemaah Islamiyah (JI) and the Abu Sayyaf Group (ASG), both with ties to Al Qaeda.

The JI is an Indonesia-based terrorist network formed in 1993 with the goal of creating a regional Islamic state spanning the countries of Indonesia, Malaysia, Singapore, southern Thailand, and the southern Philippines. The ASG was also formed in the early 1990s with the goal of creating an independent Islamic state and is considered to be a violent extremist terrorist organization that engages in kidnappings for ransom, bombings, beheadings, assassinations, and extortion with the vast majority of its victims being civilians.

During its infancy, the ASG spread terror throughout the southern Philippines by attacking Christian targets.[43] Muslim operatives were known to disguise themselves as military soldiers and raid predominantly Christian towns while indiscriminately firing at civilians, robbing businesses, and burning buildings. Their use of grenades and explosive devices accounted for hundreds of Christian deaths. Examples include a 1993 attack against a cathedral in which six were killed and another 32 wounded, a 1994 bombing which killed at least 71 people, and a 1995 large-scale attack whose casualties were 53 dead and 48 wounded.

---

[43] The Magsaysay administration promoted the resettlement of poor Christians between 1953 and 1957 from Luzon to Mindanao in order to relieve overpopulation. The migration created severe religious hostilities in the southern Philippines. Targets included, but were not limited to, churches, missionaries, and entire Christian communities.

Almost immediately after its inception, the JI likewise revealed its penchant for extreme violence. The JI planned multiple large-scale terror attacks, including the Bojinka Plot, which would have blown up twelve airliners traveling from Asia to the United States, assassinating Pope John Paul II and President Clinton during separate visits to Manila, destroying several nuclear power plants in various Western countries, and crashing an airplane into the CIA's headquarters in Virginia. Fortunately, the Bojinka plot was uncovered prior to execution, when police discovered evidence during a post-fire investigation at a Manila apartment.

Meanwhile, in contrast to the successful 1996 peace talks between the MNLF and the Ramos administration, President Estrada failed to negotiate similar terms with the MILF, which meant low-level violence continued. Moreover, the ratification of the 1999 U.S.-Philippines Visiting Forces Agreement (VFA)[44] incited the NPA to resume hostilities. Even with all of these various actors, each with its own anti-state agenda, sporadic military sweeps against the MILF and ASG did appear to temporarily weaken both extremist organizations.

F. INCREASED VIOLENCE (2000s)

During the late 1990s, the U.S. and the Philippines began to reestablish military ties. The signing of the VFA in 1999 authorized the return of U.S. military personnel to the Philippines: However, the agreement created a storm of debate about whether or not the VFA infringed on Philippine sovereignty. Regardless of the controversy, the VFA granted the Philippines an increase of U.S. Foreign Military Financing from $2 million in 2001 to $19 million in 2002. The U.S. also offered an additional $100 million worth of aid and arms,[45] whose delivery was

---

[44] It was President Estrada's intent to approve the return of American military forces to the Philippines in order to train and advise the AFP to destroy the MILF and the ASG. The VFA provides a legal framework for joint military training exercises between Philippine and U.S. armed forces.

[45] The aid and arms included a C-130 transport aircraft, eight UH-1H utility helicopters, 30,000 M-16 rifles, a Coast Guard patrol vessel, grenade launchers, mortars, and night vision goggles.

sped up due to the onset of the Global War on Terror (GWOT) in 2001. This financial and logistical assistance likely contributed to the AFP's success in combating Muslim rebels in the southern Philippines; during the last few months of 2001, the AFP killed over 100 members of the ASG and captured scores more, including individuals who claimed to be part of the Al Qaeda network.

In addition to financial and logistical support, the GWOT brought U.S. military support back to the Philippines. A decade after the Philippine government required all U.S. military forces to leave the country, President Arroyo requested their return in order to help the AFP create the conditions necessary for peace, stability, and prosperity in the southern Philippines. In January 2002, the U.S. deployed approximately 1,300 soldiers, as well as a joint military task force (JTF 510) of approximately 160 Special Forces personnel, to the southern Philippines to conduct counterterrorist operations with the AFP. Joint Task Force 510 was re-designated as the Joint Special Operations Task Force – Philippines (JSOTF-P) in the summer of 2002, and continues to be responsible for a variety of missions to include civic action programs (medical, dental, veterinary, engineer), subject matter expert programs (e.g., marksmanship and small unit tactics), intelligence sharing, and combat advising. Worth noting is that the presence of American soldiers prompted an explosion of protests against President Arroyo based on the Philippine constitution's exclusion of foreign armed forces from conducting combat operations on Philippine soil.[46]

Despite being officially limited to a non-combat role, JSOTF-P actions appeared to help neutralize insurgent efforts by "winning the hearts and minds" of the local populace: However, in the latter months of 2002, a spike in bombings and attacks that claimed the lives of hundreds of civilians and Filipino soldiers, led to U.S. personnel being restricted to their camps, forcing them to focus primarily on civic action missions.

---

[46] Although U.S. soldiers are not permitted to accompany AFP combat patrols, they are allowed to carry weapons and return fire if they are attacked.

Although U.S. Armed Forces returned to the field as combat advisors in 2004 and greatly contributed to successes against terrorist organizations, the overall trend in the 2000s seen to favor the insurgents. The MNLF, for example, conducted a series of direct confrontations with government troops in 2001, resulting in nearly 150 deaths; it executed a complex coordinated attack against three army camps and a military convoy in 2005 resulting in more than 20 deaths; and it continued to clash with the AFP in 2007, leaving more than 16 soldiers dead. During the past decade, the MNLF amplified its attacks by incorporating indirect fires and kidnappings for ransom. Mortar attacks have killed numerous military and police personnel: Of course, civilians have accounted for the majority of casualties inflicted by the Muslim group. Hostage taking is another favorite MNLF operation. The group made headlines in 2001 when it took 50 civilians hostage, and then again in 2007 when it captured an AFP general, 19 of his aides, and a prominent government official.

The MILF also increased its hostilities over the past decade. Several broken ceasefire agreements and continued failed peace talks triggered the militant organization to respond with violent action. For example, in December 2000, Islamic rebels conducted a series of complex bombing attacks known as the Rizal Day bombings[47] that took the lives of at least 22 people and wounded more than 100 others. Islamic rebels also initiated two bomb attacks against the AFP in 2003, killing 38 people and injuring several others. The MILF gained the attention of the Philippine government through these and other violent actions, including a 2005 attack against two AFP outposts where at least six soldiers were killed, a 2006 assassination attempt of a governor that resulted in the death of six people, a 2006 lethal attack against two police Ranger Scouts, and a 2007 ambush that killed 14 marines (ten of whom were found decapitated and mutilated).

---

[47] The Rizal Day bombings occurred on a national holiday, which commemorates the martyrdom of the country's national hero, Jose Rizal. The bombings occurred in five separate locations around Metro Manila, all within an hour of each other.

Hostilities continued to escalate in 2008 when a Philippine Supreme Court ruling overturned an agreement between the state and the MILF that would have allowed the insurgent group to widen its existing autonomous region. The MILF immediately resumed hostilities by seizing 15 Christian-controlled towns, burning homes, and killing civilians. Although the Islamic group attributed the atrocities to rogue field commanders, the MILF was still held responsible for the killing spree that led to more than 100 deaths over a two-month period.

The ASG also increased its violent operations in the 2000s. Under new leadership, this extremist organization intensified its use of bombing attacks. For example, the Superferry bombing in 2004 resulted in over 100 deaths and missing persons, and although the 2005 Valentine's Day bombings only took the lives of 12 individuals, they injured nearly 150 innocent civilians in three separate cities.

Although the ASG conduted the majority of its attacks against civilians (Westerners and non-Muslims), it has not stopped targeting the AFP and American military forces. For instance, an ASG ambush in 2007 gained much attention when ten of the fourteen Filipino soldiers who were killed were beheaded. The ASG also gained additional notoriety in 2009 when an IED killed two U.S. Special Forces soldiers who were on a routine convoy. This incident put the ASG back into the international spotlight and highlighted their increased use of IEDs and VBIEDs.

Although the ASG conducts various kinds of attacks, the terrorist group is widely known for its successful kidnapping operations. It proved its capabilities in 2000 when operatives traveled beyond the Philippines to take 21 people hostage (19 foreigners) from a Malaysian resort and transported them back to the southern Philippines. A year later, Muslim operatives took 20 people hostage (including three Americans) from a Philippine resort, ending with the decapitation of one hostage. That same year, a priest and three teachers were found to have been tortured following their kidnap. Then, in 2001 the ASG kidnapped an American missionary couple, Martin and Gracia Burnham. This particular kidnapping served as a pretext, in conjunction with the war on terror, for a build up of U.S. military advisors to direct AFP efforts to rescue the Burnhams and seek the total elimination of the ASG.

Jemaah Islamiyah also drew significant attention. Although the Islamic group is based in Indonesia, it is considered a significant threat to stability in the Philippines. In December 2000, JI conducted a series of bombing attacks in Manila that took the lives of 22 people and injured over 100 more. In 2002, an American soldier was killed by a nail-bomb outside a bar in the southern city of Zamboanga on the Island of Mindanao.

Outside the Philippines, JI demonstrated its ability to inflict significant numbers of casualties. In 2000, JI also attempted to assassinate the Philippine ambassador to Indonesia. Although the ambassador escaped from being murdered, two people were killed and 20 others were injured. Also in 2000, JI conducted anti-Christian campaigns in both Indonesia and the Philippines. The extremist group was responsible for the Christmas Eve bombings in Indonesia that targeted churches in Jakarta and eight other cities. The bombings resulted in 18 deaths, numerous injuries, and the destruction of more than 12 churches. In 2002, JI executed a coordinated bombing attack on the predominantly Hindu island of Bali, killing over 200 people and injuring more than 300, most of them foreign tourists. In 2003, JI carried out a car bombing in front of a Marriott Hotel in Jakarta killing 12 individuals and injuring at least 150. In 2004, the terrorist group carried out another car bombing in Jakarta outside the Australian embassy, killing at least nine people, wounding another 182, and damaging several other embassies and nearby office buildings. In 2005, JI conducted a series of bombings in Bali similar to the 2002 bombings; these attacks took the lives of 26 people and injured more than 50 in areas frequented by Western tourists. Finally, in 2009, at least eight people were killed and more than 50 injured during two near simultaneous explosions at the Ritz-Carlton and Marriott hotels in Jakarta (seven of the eight people killed were foreigners).

Although the majority of JI attacks have been outside the borders of the Philippines, its use of the Philippines for training camps and staging bases pose significant security risks to the Philippines and the entire Southeast Asian region.

G.　SUMMARY

Despite law enforcement success and successful military operations, the U.S. military-backed counterinsurgency/counterterrorism campaign continues to fall short of completely eradicating insurgent activities. Even after high-profile leaders are killed or captured, insurgent organizations remain capable of inflicting damage to both military and civilian targets. Insurgent activity in the Philippines exists thanks to the presence of several insurgent organizations and the threat they pose when joining forces or mutually supporting one another.

Although President Arroyo asserted that she considers JI to be the greatest threat to stability in the Philippines,[48] it is the affiliation among all the groups that make counterinsurgency efforts so difficult. Whereas the MILF continues to provide training and safe havens to the other groups, JI contributes vital links between Al Qaeda and the other organizations through recruiting, indoctrination, financing, and operations. The ASG, meanwhile, has evolved into nothing more than a criminal gang willing to conduct any number of terror operations for money. Each group also has been linked separately to Al Qaeda, which has financially supported various insurgent activities with the goal of extending Islamic influence throughout Southeast Asia. Also, despite the fact that each of these groups conducts acts of violence, only JI and ASG are on the U.S. State Department list of foreign terrorist organizations, the MILF and MNLF are not.

---

[48] Simon Elegant, "Elevated Threat," *Time,*
http://www.time.com/time/magazine/article/0,9171,501031103-526545,00.html, 2010).

V. CONCLUSION

In reviewing our three case studies, an argument can be made there are several reasons why the United States should not want to continue its presence in the Philippines: First, as in Colombia, the U.S. has spent more than 50 years helping the Philippines combat protracted insurgencies with no clear victory in sight; second, as with the 1999 U.S.-backed Plan Colombia, U.S.-Philippine efforts in the war on terror in the southern Philippines have yet to establish necessary conditions for handling multiple insurgencies simultaneously; third, in contrast to the Philippines and Colombia, what we saw in Sri Lanka was an instance of a country successfully countering its insurgency with no American assistance.   At the same time we want to review why the U.S. should not continue its presence in the Philippines, we also want to raise the question, "What would happen if the U.S. withdrew from the Philippines?" More specifically, what would be the dangers if insurgent organizations unified in the absence of a U.S. presence, and what negative influence could external actors have if the U.S. chooses to withdraw from the Philippines? By considering these questions, we aim to demonstrate that, in fact, the U.S. presence is absolutely necessary in the Philippines.

A.   DANGERS OF INSURGENT UNIFICATION

One of the dangers of the U.S. not maintaining a presence in the Philippines is the potential threat of several insurgent groups uniting and posing a larger threat to the stability of the country. As indicated earlier, Islamic insurgent organizations operating in the southern Philippines already have historic relations with one another; persistent U.S.-backed AFP efforts have only modestly decreased insurgent effectiveness. Sri Lanka is an example of what can happen if individual insurgent groups are not adequately controlled. In the late 1960s and early 1970s, prior to the official start of the Sri Lankan war, there were at least seven burgeoning revolutionary organizations that challenged the authority of the government in Colombo. Failure of the Sri Lankan government to combat these individual groups allowed for their eventual unification and the formation of a larger more powerful insurgent organization known as the New Tamil Tigers, or the LTTE. This new organization would go on to conduct a violent 26-year-long insurgency. Without a U.S. presence in the Philippines, a similar situation could occur, leading to the emergence of a more effective and formidable group of unified insurgent organizations than any the Philippines has yet seen.

Another danger of not maintaining a U.S. presence in the Philippines is allowing domestic insurgent groups the opportunity to play a role in a much larger network of violent actors elsewhere in the world. As noted earlier, Islamic insurgent organizations already have various ties to Al Qaeda, and by our *not* disrupting guerrilla operations, these groups could even more successfully network with each other to further Al Qaeda's radical Muslim movement calling for a global jihad. The LTTE offers an example of an insurgent group that influenced other groups on an unprecedented scale at an international level. The LTTE was known to provide combat and explosives training to the MILF and ASG in the Philippines, the Al Ummah terrorist group in India, and rebel fighters in Afghanistan. The LTTE also reportedly had links to the FARC in Colombia, as well as to other groups in countries like Lebanon, France, Myanmar, Thailand, and Cambodia. If the U.S. chose to withdraw from the Philippines and not help the AFP combat violent insurgent groups, then a similar situation could arise. Rebel groups in the southern Philippines could either influence the Southeast Asian region indirectly through their deeds, or could become a conduit for achieving Al Qaeda's goal of creating a new Islamic caliphate.

B.   INFLUENCE OF EXTERNAL ACTORS

If the U.S. chooses not to maintain a presence in the Philippines, it also risks the chance of a competing global power, whose interests may not be in agreement with the U.S., replacing it as an influential external actor. In the case of Colombia, the absence of an American presence would likely encourage countries like Venezuela and Cuba to promptly reestablish a partnership that could have long-term adverse consequences for the U.S. These partnerships, for instance, could result in the legalization and subsequent taxation of the drug industry. The revenue could subsequently support Venezuela's and Cuba's anti-American efforts.[49] Additionally, Colombia could stand the risk of losing its current democratic system to that of Venezuela's more-authoritarian style democracy. In Sri Lanka, our lack of participation presented an opportunity for the Chinese government to supplement the Sri Lankan government with weapons and ammunition to help eradicate the LTTE. This partnership in turn created an opportunity for China to build and operate a three-phased harbor intended to be a leading intermediary harbor in the Indian Ocean Zone. Once completed, this harbor will service ships traveling along one of the world's busiest shipping lines (the east-west shipping route), making it the largest port in South Asia.

As China continues to increase its influence in Sri Lanka, recent studies indicate that its influence is also rising in the Philippines. Although the U.S. remains the dominant foreign military, political, economic, and cultural influence in the Philippines, "Some U.S. and Philippine policy makers have expressed concern regarding China's growing 'soft power' and the perceived lack of U.S. comprehensive attention to Philippine and regional issues."[50] It is critical that the U.S. continue its support of democratic allies. Without continued support, countries like Sri Lanka may revert from a democratic style of government to one based on an authoritarian-type rule of law, as seen in communist countries. In addition to the U.S. presence being able to help deter influence from potential competitors like China, there are also rogues like North Korea who could step into the vacuum.

---

[49] Drug Reform Coordination Network (DRCNet, http://stopthedrugwar.org/chronicle-old/438/gaviriadiaz.shtml.

[50] Congressional Research Service, http://www.fas.org/sgp/crs/row/RL33233.pdf.

C.   WAY AHEAD

There are many lessons that can be gleaned from Plan Colombia and from Sri Lanka's extermination of the LTTE.   The U.S.-backed Colombian initiative contributed to a significant reduction in FARC numbers and subsequently diminished FARC's ability to mount a substantial offensive operation against the Colombian government. The successes in Colombia are a result of the increase in U.S. military aid. Specifically, the U.S. provided air platforms to enable Colombia to move deeper into FARC-held territory, as well as more specialized training directed at further developing this deep jungle penetration capability.

The U.S.-backed Plan Colombia was more than just a program to defeat the guerrilla movement and illicit drug activities in Colombia. The plan was developed in such a manner as to democratically unify all the citizens of Colombia, in keeping with international human right laws, to create a stable, more equitable economy. Additionally, the plan allowed the U.S. to maintain its long-term relationship with the Colombian military, and thereby preserve a strategic capability in South America.

This concept can be utilized as a framework to assist in uniting the people of the Philippines. As was the case in Colombia, the contentiousness in the Philippines is not in the capital or major cities, but in the external provinces of Visayas and Mindanao. By instituting a plan similar to the one used in Colombia, the U.S.-backed Philippine government could create an opportunity for improved political, social, and economical stability, while collectively consolidating its force structure to defeat the insurgencies that plague the southern provinces.

If, on the other hand, the Philippine government chose to confront its insurgent groups in the manner in which Sri Lanka destroyed the LTTE, inevitable rights violation would certainly ensue. Though this would not be a decision that would at all be popular internationally, the U.S. could choose to continue supporting the Philippine government, much as China aided Sri Lanka.

The U.S. could provide the means (funding, technology, weapons, and training), but not the forces to help the Philippine military defeat its insurgent adversaries. However, this initiative would require the U.S. to turn a "blind eye" to the predictable atrocities.

Far better for all concerned would be for the Philippine government to maintain its current partnership with the U.S. and seek to develop a more definitive program that addresses the internal issues within its borders. Failure to do so could result in chaos and turmoil, with the insurgents in the south fracturing the nation and straining the Philippines' relationship with the West. By maintaining its partnership with the U.S., the Philippines is more likely to prevent the spread of the insurgent ideology from Mindanao, which will also keep it a vital member of the global community in good standing.

THIS PAGE INTENTIONALLY LEFT BLANK

LIST OF REFERENCES

Conner, Jr., Robert J. "Defeating the Modern Asymmetric Threat." Naval Postgraduate School. (2002). http://www.dtic.mil/cgi-bin/GetTRDoc?AD=ADA405818&Location=U2&doc=GetTRDoc.pdf.

Das, R.N. "China's Foray into Sri Lanka and India's Response." Institute for Defense Studies & Analyses. (August 5, 2010). http://www.idsa.in/idsacomments/ChinasForayintoSriLankaandIndiasResponse_rndas_050810.

Earth Times. "Military Claims Counter-insurgency Success in Philippines." http://www.earthtimes.org/articles/news/335455,claims-counter-insurgency-success-philippines.html.

Elegant, Simon. "Elevated Threat." *Time.* http://www.time.com/time/magazine/article/0,9171,501031103-526545,00.html.

Federation of American Scientists. http://www.fas.org.

Global Security. http://www.globalsecurity.org.

"Government Yet to Pay Compensation to July '83 Victims." *Daily News.* (March 30, 2004). http://www.dailynews.lk/2004/03/30/new14.html.

"IPKF in Sri Lanka – India's Vietnam." Sri Lanka Virtual Library. (March 2000). http://www.lankalibrary.com/pol/india3.htm.

Jane's Information Group. http://jtic.janes.com

Kaperak, Mark A. "Battle of Wills: Accepting Stalemate in Internal Wars." Naval Postgraduate School. (December 2009). http://www.dtic.mil/cgi-bin/GetTRDoc?AD=ADA514265&Location=U2&doc=GetTRDoc.pdf.

Kaplan, Robert D. "To Catch a Tiger." *The Atlantic.* (July 1, 2009). http://www.theatlantic.com/doc/200907u/tamil-tigers-counterinsurgency.

Kingsbury, Damien. "Sri Lanka." In *Hot Spot: Asia and Oceania* by Clinton Fernandes. Westport: Greenwood Press, 2008.

LeGrand, Catherine. "Agrarian Antecedents of the Violence." *Violence in Colombia: The Contemporary Crisis in Historical Perspective. Ed.* Charles Berquist, Richard Penaranda, Gonzalo Sanchez. Wilmington: A Scholarly Resources Inc. Imprint, 1992.

Marcella, Garbriel. "The United States and Colombia: The Journey from Ambiguity to Strategic Clarity." (May 2003). http://www.strategicstudiesinstitute.army.mil/pubs/display.cfm?pubID=10.

O'Ballance, Edgar. *The Cyanide War: Tamil Insurrection in Sri Lanka, 1973-1988.* London: Brassey's, 1989.

"Prehistoric Basis for the Rise of Civilisation in Sri Lanka and Southern India." Sri Lanka Virtual Library. (2004). http://www.lankalibrary.com/geo/prehistory.htm.

"President Kumaratunga's speech on the 21st Anniversary of 'Black July,' Presidential Secretariat, Colombo, July 23, 2004." South Asia Terrorism Portal. (July 23, 2004). http://www.satp.org/satporgtp/countries/shrilanka/document/papers/BlackJuly2004.htm.

Ramirez, Maria Clemencia. "Maintaining Democracy in Colombia through Political Exclusion, State of Exception, Counterinsurgency, and Dirty War." *Violent Democracies in Latin America*. Ed. Enrique Desmond Arias and Daniel M. Goldstein. Durham: Duke University Press, 2010.

Simons, Geoff. *Colombia: A Brutal History.* London: SAQI, 2004.

Smith, Chris. "The Eelam Endgame?" International Affairs, 83 (2007): 1. http://onlinelibrary.wiley.com/doi/10.1111/j.1468-2346.2007.00603.x/pdf.

"Sri Lanka." Central Intelligence Agency: The World Factbook. https://www.cia.gov/search?q=sri+lanka&x=0&y=0&site=CIA&output=xml_no_dtd&client=CIA&myAction=%2Fsearch&proxystylesheet=CIA&submitMethod=get.

"Sri Lanka." Encyclopedia of the Nations. http://www.nationsencyclopedia.com/Asia-and-Oceania/Sri-Lanka.html.

"The Sri Lankan Conflict." Council on Foreign Relations. (May 18, 2009). http://www.cfr.org/publication/11407/sri_lankan_conflict.html.

"The Sri Lanka Project: Massacre in the Hills." *British Refugee Council: No. 153.* (October 2000). http://brcslproject.gn.apc.org/slmonitor/october2000/mass.html.

"Sri Lanka: The End of the Tigers." STRATFOR Global Intelligence. http://www.stratfor.com.libproxy.nps.edu/analysis/20090518_sri_lanka_end_tigers.

Stokke, Kristian. "Building the Tamil Eelam State: Emerging State Institutions and Forms of Governance in LTTE-controlled Areas in Sri Lanka." *Third World Quarterly,* 27 no. 6 (2006).

Templar, Robert. "War Without End." *International Herald Tribune.* (July 21, 2009). http://www.nytimes.com/2009/07/22/opinion/22iht-edtempler.html.

Veillette, Connie. "Plan Colombia: A Progress Report." Report for Congress, (June 22, 2005). http://www.fas.org/sgp/crs/row/RL32774.pdf.

"Worldwide Incidents Tracking System." National Counterterrorism Center. http://wits-classic.nctc.gov/.

www.ingramcontent.com/pod-product-compliance
Lightning Source LLC
Chambersburg PA
CBHW080615290526
45790CB00007B/2784